STRENGTHS EXPLORATION WORKBOOK

Strength 1:

Strength 2:

Strength 3:

Strength 4:

Strength 5:

STRENGTHS EXPLORATION WORKBOOK

What to do After you get your List of Strengths

Disclosure

This workbook is designed to be used in instructor led workshops and may not be suitable for individual use.

Most strength based assessment organizations do not certify any external consultants to interpret their results. As such, the information you receive during a strength focused workshop has not been approved and is not sanctioned or endorsed by the strength based assessment provider in any way. Opinions, views, and interpretations of the results are solely the beliefs of the instructor.

Neither the strength based assessment provider nor the publisher are a party to any agreement with you or the instructor and shall have no liability whatsoever with respect to any of the services that are subject to the contract. The services provided under that contract are not provided, licensed, warrantied or sponsored by the strength based assessment provider or the publisher.

ISBN: 978-0692655764
Published by Focal Star Publishing, California, USA

Table of Contents

Success is achieved by developing our strengths, not by eliminating our weaknesses.

- Marilyn vos Savant

INTRODUCTION

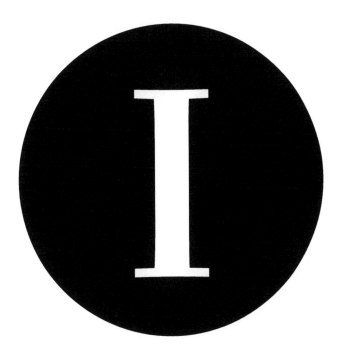

There are many resources to help you minimize your weaknesses, however, research shows that you can get a greater return from the same investment when you focus on improving your Strengths.

The focus of this workbook is to help you to understand your Strengths, identify how they work in your life already, and create a plan to maximize those Strengths.

Our first instinct whenever we are graded, evaluated or assessed is to quickly scan through what you did well and to find where you messed up. Everyone wants to know where their biggest faults are so that they can pour more time and attention into fixing themselves.

One of the reasons for the success of Strength Based training is that at its foundation is the truth that we all possess valuable qualities. There is potential inside everyone and when we connect that talent with skills, knowledge and purpose you've got a Strength that breathes life into that person and those around them.

The key is to move past the concept that the only way to improve is to fix our faults. We need to take ownership of our future by actively engaging in a process to become more of who we are destined to be. There is a rich potential just waiting to be discovered. You've started the journey by engaging in this workshop. Are you ready to move through the exercises and do the extra work it suggests? Or will you simply sit back and wait for this *Strengths* fad to pass, all the while knowing that others are coming alive through this process?

The research into understanding your Strengths has set a foundation upon which millions have come to understand they were designed with giftings, abilities and talents that were meant to be discovered, honed and shared.

Now is the time to move to a new level of understanding. Reach beyond your results to a place where you work in your Strengths everyday.

The following pages include numerous blank areas for a reason. They were meant to be used, both with introspective time and in interactive activities, to move your understanding of Strengths to a whole new level. With time and practice, you can develop your Strengths and dramatically improve your performance.

Even if you don't complete every aspect of this workbook during the workshop, please feel free to step into the other sections. Although not all of them are self-explanatory, there are several sections that you will be able to easily walk through and further develop an understanding and application of your Strengths.

In addition, there are numerous sections that require introspective time that is not easy to complete during a workshop. You may only be able to start a section with just one of your Strengths before the group moves on to another section. To maximize your learning, complete the whole section in its entirety, working on your other Strengths as well.

This will help you extend your understanding and develop your ability to spend more time in your Strengths, letting the real you happily charge forward into a brighter tomorrow.

Too many people overvalue what they are not and undervalue what they are.

- Malcom Forbes

MY STRENGTHS REFERENCE

This section creates an easy to find overview of key elements about your Strengths. After you review all of the Individual Strengths, complete the information about your top Strengths by completing the My Top Strengths page.

Complete the Individual Strength Statement page after completing the Individual Strength Statements section.

My Top Strengths

1

Strength:

Summary:

-
-
-

2

Strength:

Summary:

-
-
-

3

Strength:

Summary:

-
-
-

4

Strength:

Summary:

-
-
-

5

Strength:

Summary:

-
-
-

Individual Strength Statements

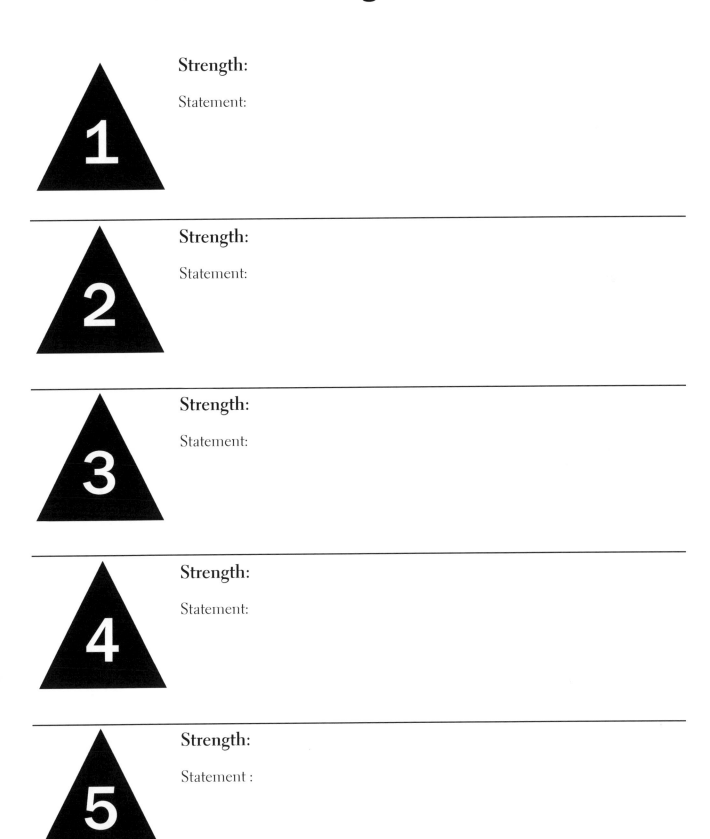

Strength:

Statement:

Strength:

Statement:

Strength:

Statement:

Strength:

Statement:

Strength:

Statement :

What lies behind us and what lies before us are tiny matters compared to what lies within us.

- Ralph Waldo Emerson

STRENGTHS REVIEW

There is more to understanding Strengths than just learning about your top few. What they are, how to leverage them and how to effectively work with others is equally important. As you learn about the Strengths system, this area provides unobstructed space to take notes and jot down observations that will deepen your understanding.

Notes:

Find your own 'sweet spot'. Take your talents and enjoy them, share them, expand them.

- Kofi Awoonor

INDIVIDUAL STRENGTHS

It is critically important to understand your own Strengths before you can effectively leverage them to improve performance and satisfaction in your life. The following pages provide room for you to take notes while the workshop leader reviews all of the different Strengths.

It is highly recommended that you take notes on all of the Strengths, not just your own. This will provide you with a resource to review in the future when dealing with others. There are millions of people out there and very few, if any, will have the exact same combination of Strengths that you have.

Understanding each of the Strengths will enable you to deepen your understanding of how to best work with and connect with others.

Strength Name:

Example:

Others with this Strength:

Summary:

Strength Name:

Example:

Others with this Strength:

Summary:

Strength Name:

Example:

Others with this Strength:

Summary:

Strength Name:

Example:

Others with this Strength:

Summary:

Strength Name:

Example:

Others with this Strength:

Summary:

Strength Name:

Example:

Others with this Strength:

Summary:

Strength Name:

Example:

Others with this Strength:

Summary:

Strength Name:

Example:

Others with this Strength:

Summary:

Strength Name:

Example:

Others with this Strength:

Summary:

Strength Name:

Example:

Others with this Strength:

Summary:

Strength Name:

Example:

Others with this Strength:

Summary:

Strength Name:

Example:

Others with this Strength:

Summary:

Strength Name:

Example:

Others with this Strength:

Summary:

Strength Name:

Example:

Others with this Strength:

Summary:

Strength Name:

Example:

Others with this Strength:

Summary:

Strength Name:

Example:

Others with this Strength:

Summary:

Strength Name:

Example:

Others with this Strength:

Summary:

Strength Name:

Example:

Others with this Strength:

Summary:

Strength Name:

Example:

Others with this Strength:

Summary:

Strength Name:

Example:

Others with this Strength:

Summary:

Strength Name:

Example:

Others with this Strength:

Summary:

Strength Name:

Example:

Others with this Strength:

Summary:

Strength Name:

Example:

Others with this Strength:

Summary:

Strength Name:

Example:

Others with this Strength:

Summary:

Strength Name:

Example:

Others with this Strength:

Summary:

Strength Name:

Example:

Others with this Strength:

Summary:

Strength Name:

Example:

Others with this Strength:

Summary:

Strength Name:

Example:

Others with this Strength:

Summary:

Strength Name:

Example:

Others with this Strength:

Summary:

Strength Name:

Example:

Others with this Strength:

Summary:

Strength Name:

Example:

Others with this Strength:

Summary:

Strength Name:

Example:

Others with this Strength:

Summary:

Strength Name:

Example:

Others with this Strength:

Summary:

Strength Name:

Example:

Others with this Strength:

Summary:

Figure out what you really love doing and use your strengths on a daily basis.

- Tom Rath

UNDERSTANDING YOUR STRENGTHS

Your Strengths are adaptive and have different expressions based upon the needs of the situation. This exercise isolates the use of each Strength into one of four roles that you live out. Pick the roles that you spend the most time interacting in. This could include employee, student, spouse, parent, friend, community leader, coach, small group member or any number of areas of your life. Think about each role one at a time and how every one of your Strengths either has or could have played out to help you maximize the benefit you add to each role.

List your Strengths on the left, then list out four roles you are in. Briefly describe how you see each Strength playing within each of the roles you spend most of your time in.

	Role 1	Role 2
Strength 1		
Strength 2		
Strength 3		
Strength 4		
Strength 5		

List your Strengths on the left, then list out four roles you are in. Briefly describe how you see each Strength playing within each of the roles you spend most of your time in.

	Role 3	Role 4
Strength 1		
Strength 2		
Strength 3		
Strength 4		
Strength 5		

When we think about our strengths, we are strong. When w think about our weaknesses, we are weak.

- *Pete Cohen*

STRENGTHS MISUNDERSTOOD

When others don't understand our strengths they often apply labels to try to describe their limited experience with us. List your Strengths and then name the misperceptions others have of that Strength. Finally, list what you really want them to understand about your Strengths.

This exercise allows you begin to separate the good aspects of your Strengths from the misperceptions and labels that others apply when Strengths are misunderstood.

List each of your Strengths below and after thinking about each one, write out the names and labels others have used to describe the misunderstood potential of that strength. Then in the last column describe what you would want them to know instead. This should include what value you bring when you successfully are living out each Strength.

#	Strength	Titles Given when Misunderstood	Who I Really Am

You can run a business any way you like, but you'll run it better if you build it around your strengths

- Duncan Bannatyne

OPTIMUM VS. OVERUSED

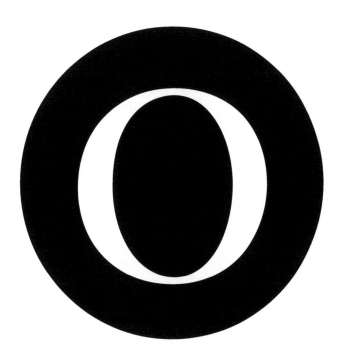

Just as too much of a good thing can be bad for you, so can displaying too much of your Strengths become a shortcoming.

Overusing your Strengths keeps others from experiencing your Strengths at their best. When overused, Strengths become weapons that depreciate relational capital and hurt relationships. Other titles given when Strengths are over used are Overplayed, Shadow Side, Basement, along with a few others. In this workbook we will use the term Overused to describe when a Strength is overextended and continued application no longer adds value to the situation as a whole.

Take a moment and think about how your Strengths may have been overused in the past. What happened to the task? What happened to the relationships?

Take a few moments and describe 2 or 3 occasions when one or more of your Strengths were overused. Include what happened to the task or the relationships around each occasion.

Examples of Strengths Overused:

1.

2.

3.

Write a brief description that describes what happens when your Strengths are at their Optimum and again when they are Overused. This can serve as a reference point for understanding why things are not going the way you would like and help to bring you back on track to the optimum levels.

Strength	Optimum	Overused
1.		
2.		
3.		
4.		
5.		

Accept yourself, your strengths, your weaknesses, your truths, and know what tools you have to fulfill your purpose.

- *Steve Maraboli*

INDIVIDUAL STRENGTH STATEMENTS

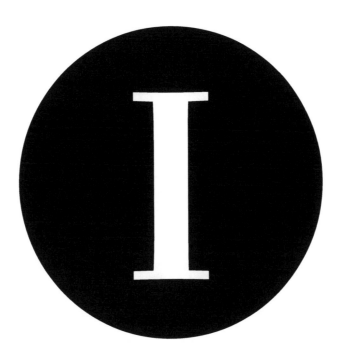

Personalized declarations of how each Strength
works in your life enabling you to become
powerful, **effective** and more **alive**.

The creation of your Individual Strength Statements starts with the focus on each Strength on its own. This allows a more intimate understanding of how each Strength works in your life with the focus of how to maximize it. This process takes some time, and is often spread out over different periods.

Powerful

Strength 1:

With your #1 Strength in mind, complete the sentence below 2 or 3 times to help identify the building blocks of your Strength Statement.

Think about activities over the last week, month and year where you felt **powerful** either during or just after completing the activity.

I feel most powerful when I...
1.
2.
3.

Identify all of the Who, What, Where, When, Why components of each statement above. Circle the components that repeat the most.

WHO:

WHAT:

WHERE:

WHEN:

WHY:

Effective

Strength 1:

With your #1 Strength in mind, complete the sentence below 2 or 3 times to help identify the building blocks of your Strength Statement.

Think about activities over the last week, month and year where you felt **effective** either during or just after completing it.

	I feel most effective when I...
1.	
2.	
3.	

Identify all of the Who, What, Where, When, Why components of each statement above. Circle the components that repeat the most.

WHO:

WHAT:

WHERE:

WHEN:

WHY:

Alive

Strength 1:

With your #1 Strength in mind, complete the sentence below 2 or 3 times to help identify the building blocks of your Strength Statement.

Think about activities over the last week, month and year where you felt **alive** either during or just after completing it.

I feel most alive when I...
1.
2.
3.

Identify all of the Who, What, Where, When, Why components of each statement above. Circle the components that repeat the most.

WHO:

WHAT:

WHERE:

WHEN:

WHY:

Strength Statement

Strength 1:

It is now time to combine the sentences from each of the last three pages into just two or three. You will want to start with the sentences you feel the most energy and excitement behind. Keep in mind the most common Who, What, Where, When, Why components which may need to be woven into the summary statements.

Once complete, re-write the statement on the My Strengths Reference section in the front of the workbook under the Individual Strength Statement section.

Powerful

2

Strength 2:

With your #2 Strength in mind, complete the sentence below 2 or 3 times to help identify the building blocks of your Strength Statement.

Think about activities over the last week, month and year where you felt **powerful** either during or just after completing it.

I feel most powerful when I...
1.
2.
3.

Identify all of the Who, What, Where, When, Why components of each statement above. Circle the components that repeat the most.

WHO:

WHAT:

WHERE:

WHEN:

WHY:

Effective

Strength 2:

With your #2 Strength in mind, complete the sentence below 2 or 3 times to help identify the building blocks of your Strength Statement.

Think about activities over the last week, month and year where you felt **effective** either during or just after completing it.

I feel most effective when I...
1.
2.
3.

Identify all of the Who, What, Where, When, Why components of each statement above. Circle the components that repeat the most.

WHO:

WHAT:

WHERE:

WHEN:

WHY:

Alive

2

Strength 2:

With your #2 Strength in mind, complete the sentence below 2 or 3 times to help identify the building blocks of your Strength Statement.

Think about activities over the last week, month and year where you felt **alive** either during or just after completing it.

I feel most alive when I...
1.
2.
3.

Identify all of the Who, What, Where, When, Why components of each statement above. Circle the components that repeat the most.

WHO:

WHAT:

WHERE:

WHEN:

WHY:

Strength Statement

Strength 2:

It is now time to combine the sentences from each of the last three pages into just two or three. You will want to start with the sentences you feel the most energy and excitement behind. Keep in mind the most common Who, What, Where, When, Why components which may need to be woven into the summary statements.

Once complete, re-write the statement on the My Strengths Reference section in the front of the workbook under the Individual Strength Statement section.

Powerful

3

Strength 3:

With your #3 Strength in mind, complete the sentence below 2 or 3 times to help identify the building blocks of your Strength Statement.

Think about activities over the last week, month and year where you felt **powerful** either during or just after completing it.

I feel most powerful when I...
1.
2.
3.

Identify all of the Who, What, Where, When, Why components of each statement above. (Circle) the components that repeat the most.

WHO:

WHAT:

WHERE:

WHEN:

WHY:

Effective

Strength 3:

With your #3 Strength in mind, complete the sentence below 2 or 3 times to help identify the building blocks of your Strength Statement.

Think about activities over the last week, month and year where you felt **effective** either during or just after completing it.

I feel most effective when I...
1.
2.
3.

Identify all of the Who, What, Where, When, Why components of each statement above. Circle the components that repeat the most.

WHO:

WHAT:

WHERE:

WHEN:

WHY:

Alive

3

Strength 3:

With your #3 Strength in mind, complete the sentence below 2 or 3 times to help identify the building blocks of your Strength Statement.

Think about activities over the last week, month and year where you felt **alive** either during or just after completing it.

I feel most alive when I...
1.
2.
3.

Identify all of the Who, What, Where, When, Why components of each statement above. (Circle) the components that repeat the most.

WHO:

WHAT:

WHERE:

WHEN:

WHY:

Strength Statement

Strength 3:

It is now time to combine the sentences from each of the last three pages into just two or three. You will want to start with the sentences you feel the most energy and excitement behind. Keep in mind the most common Who, What, Where, When, Why components which may need to be woven into the summary statements.

Once complete, re-write the statement on the My Strengths Reference section in the front of the workbook under the Individual Strength Statement section.

Powerful

Strength 4:

With your #4 Strength in mind, complete the sentence below 2 or 3 times to help identify the building blocks of your Strength Statement.

Think about activities over the last week, month and year where you felt **powerful** either during or just after completing it.

I feel most powerful when I...
1.
2.
3.

Identify all of the Who, What, Where, When, Why components of each statement above. Circle the components that repeat the most.

WHO:

WHAT:

WHERE:

WHEN:

WHY:

Effective

Strength 4:

With your #4 Strength in mind, complete the sentence below 2 or 3 times to help identify the building blocks of your Strength Statement.

Think about activities over the last week, month and year where you felt **effective** either during or just after completing it.

	I feel most effective when I...
1.	
2.	
3.	

Identify all of the Who, What, Where, When, Why components of each statement above. Circle the components that repeat the most.

WHO:

WHAT:

WHERE:

WHEN:

WHY:

Alive

4

Strength 4:

With your #4 Strength in mind, complete the sentence below 2 or 3 times to help identify the building blocks of your Strength Statement.

Think about activities over the last week, month and year where you felt **alive** either during or just after completing it.

	I feel most alive when I...
1.	
2.	
3.	

Identify all of the Who, What, Where, When, Why components of each statement above. (Circle) the components that repeat the most.

WHO:

WHAT:

WHERE:

WHEN:

WHY:

Strength Statement

Strength 4:

It is now time to combine the sentences from each of the last three pages into just two or three. You will want to start with the sentences you feel the most energy and excitement behind. Keep in mind the most common Who, What, Where, When, Why components which may need to be woven into the summary statements.

Once complete, re-write the statement on the My Strengths Reference section in the front of the workbook under the Individual Strength Statement section.

Powerful

Strength 5:

With your #5 Strength in mind, complete the sentence below 2 or 3 times to help identify the building blocks of your Strength Statement.

Think about activities over the last week, month and year where you felt **powerful** either during or just after completing it.

I feel most powerful when I...	
1.	
2.	
3.	

Identify all of the Who, What, Where, When, Why components of each statement above. Circle the components that repeat the most.

WHO:

WHAT:

WHERE:

WHEN:

WHY:

Effective

Strength 5:

With your #5 Strength in mind, complete the sentence below 2 or 3 times to help identify the building blocks of your Strength Statement.

Think about activities over the last week, month and year where you felt **effective** either during or just after completing it.

I feel most effective when I...
1.
2.
3.

Identify all of the Who, What, Where, When, Why components of each statement above. Circle the components that repeat the most.

WHO:

WHAT:

WHERE:

WHEN:

WHY:

Alive

Strength 5:

With your #5 Strength in mind, complete the sentence below 2 or 3 times to help identify the building blocks of your Strength Statement.

Think about activities over the last week, month and year where you felt **alive** either during or just after completing it.

I feel most alive when I...
1.
2.
3.

Identify all of the Who, What, Where, When, Why components of each statement above. Circle the components that repeat the most.

WHO:

WHAT:

WHERE:

WHEN:

WHY:

Strength Statement

Strength 5:

It is now time to combine the sentences from each of the last three pages into just two or three. You will want to start with the sentences you feel the most energy and excitement behind. Keep in mind the most common Who, What, Where, When, Why components which may need to be woven into the summary statements.

Once complete, re-write the statement on the My Strengths Reference section in the front of the workbook under the Individual Strength Statement section.

Just do what you do best.

- Red Auerbach

It isn't easy to keep new information at the forefront of your mind. However, if you want to reap the long-term benefits of leveraging your strengths, you need a way to remember what you are now learning. The Quick Reference is a tool that can help. Complete and post this half sheet somewhere where you will see it every day. It will be a reminder to think about your Strengths and how to use them throughout the day.

Posting a copy at work on your wall or door can be a reminder for both you and those you work with. This is especially valuable when you and your co-workers commit to help each other to continually bring improvement.

So, complete, post and keep focusing on your Strengths!

My Strengths

Name

Top Strengths

-

-

-

-

-

My Strengths

Name

Top Strengths

-

-

-

-

-

My Strengths

Name

Top Strengths

-

-

-

-

-

My Strengths

Name

Top Strengths

-

-

-

-

-

Exercise A

Exercise B

Exercise B

Made in United States
Orlando, FL
14 January 2024

42466118R00050